SUPER BOWL
FIREWORKS!

BY JAMES BUCKLEY, JR.

SCHOLASTIC INC.

New York   Toronto   London   Auckland
Sydney   Mexico City   New Delhi   Hong Kong

ISBN-13: 978-0-545-13126-1
ISBN-10: 0-545-13126-X

Published by Scholastic Inc.
SCHOLASTIC and associated logos are trademarks and/or registered trademarks of Scholastic Inc.

12 11 10 9 8 7 6 5 4 3 2   9 10 11 12 13 14/0

Cover Design by Cheung Tai
Interior Design by Rocco Melillo
Printed in U.S.A.
First Scholastic printing, July 2009

CONTENTS

FIREWORKS IN FEBRUARY!

The Super Bowl is the NFL's — heck, the sports world's! — biggest stage. On that stage, the greatest players have come through for decades. The very best players save their very best for the big day. This book takes a look at all of those ultra-highlight, super-special moments.

Did you watch Super Bowl XLIII? Was that awesome or what? Remember when that guy huffed and puffed 100 yards with an interception? Or when that one dude with the long hair went long? Or when the blimp landed on the field at halftime?

Okay, that last one didn't happen. Just making sure you were paying attention. Still, Super Bowl XLIII had more than its fair share of amazing plays. There was an awesome defensive play, a game-breaking long TD pass, and a last-minute TD grab. In between, there were awesome runs, more great passes, and some serious hits.

In this book, you'll meet all the heroes who came through when their team needed them . . . and the plays that made them famous. Plus, we'll revisit other great (and not-so-great!) moments in Super Bowl history. These are the plays that fans will be talking about when you take your own kids to the game in 2030! (Save us some popcorn, okay?) These are the plays that make fireworks go off in February (okay, January, too . . . .).

GREAT CATCHES!

Okay, everybody, go long! That's what you tell your pals when you're on the field. In the NFL, it's a bit trickier. But to make some of the most famous Super Bowl catches, great receivers did just that — they went long! Let's relive the greatest receptions in Super Bowl history!

MCGEE'S FIRST

Max McGee didn't even think he'd play in Super Bowl I. Boyd Dowler was the star receiver for the Green Bay Packers. Dowler was hurt early in the game, however. Coach Vince Lombardi called on backup Max. McGee scored the first touchdown in Super Bowl history on a 37-yard pass. He had to reach back with one hand to make the grab! He scored again in the fourth quarter after juggling the ball! Lucky Max!

SWANN DIVE

Lynn Swann only touched the football four times in Super Bowl X. However, those four touches played a huge part in Pittsburgh's 21–17 win over Dallas. The biggest catch Swann made came in the second quarter. The Steelers were near their own end zone. Terry Bradshaw launched a pass toward Swann. The receiver was tripped by a defender. As Swann fell, he kept his eyes on the ball. He tipped it, tapped it, and, as he was falling on his back, grabbed it! What a catch!

JUMPIN' JOHNSON!

A broken thumb didn't stop Butch Johnson in Super Bowl XII. The speedy receiver made a miraculous diving catch in the third quarter for a 45-yard touchdown!

GAME-WINNER

The San Francisco 49ers found themselves in an odd spot late in Super Bowl XXIII. They were behind! But with Joe Montana in charge . . . no problem. The icy-cool QB led the team on a 92-yard march. He capped it off by hitting John Taylor with a perfect 10-yard TD pass. There were only 34 seconds left. It was the first Super Bowl decided by such a late touchdown.

ONE BIG QUARTER

In Super Bowl XXII, Washington quarterback Doug Williams put on an unmatched passing show. In the space of 15 minutes he threw four touchdown passes! They went for 80, 27, 50, and 8 yards. No surprise, the Redskins won 42–10.

VERY NICE, RICE!

Everyone knew that the 49ers had an explosive offense. But what they did in Super Bowl XXIX was ridiculous! On only the third play of the game, Jerry Rice caught a 44-yard TD pass. The 'Niners were off and running. Rice was the receiving star. He nabbed two more TDs to set a Super Bowl record.

SUPER STEVE

Someone had to get Jerry Rice all those passes. That job fell to Steve Young in Super Bowl XXIX. Young had one of the best passing days in NFL history. Along with the three TDs caught by Rice, Young threw three more! His total of six scoring passes is an all-time NFL postseason record!

AIR IT OUT: PART I

Long touchdown plays are fun for everyone. The quarterback loves to toss them, receivers love to catch them. The fans love to watch them. The defense . . . oh, okay, long TDs are not so much fun for the defense.

In Super Bowl XXXI, a pair of Packers connected on a super-long play. The second quarter was barely under way when Antonio Freeman streaked down the right sideline. Brett Favre heaved the ball and 81 yards later . . . touchdown!

AIR IT OUT: PART II

The Favre-to-Freeman connection helped Green Bay win that game. But it came early. In Super Bowl XXXIV, another long TD gave one team the points it needed to win. The St. Louis Rams and Tennessee Titans were tied 16–16. Less than two minutes were left when Kurt Warner dropped back to pass. The strong-armed former grocery store clerk (really!) dropped a rainbow right into the hands of Isaac Bruce. Bruce left the defense behind to score on a 73-yard TD. The Rams' defense held on, and St. Louis won 23–16.

AIR IT OUT: PART III

The Super Bowl record for longest touchdown pass is one that the players who set it would gladly give back — if they could change the score of the game. In Super Bowl XXXVIII, Carolina's Jake Delhomme and Muhsin Muhammad hooked up on an 85-yard score. It gave the Panthers the lead . . . briefly. New England came back and ended up winning on a field goal in the final seconds.

NOT JUST QBS!

Quarterbacks don't have all the fun. In Super Bowl XL, Pittsburgh wide receiver Antwaan Randle El threw a 43-yard scoring strike to Hines Ward. The TD sealed the Steelers' 21–10 win.

ESCAPE!

Ever hear of Harry Houdini? He was a famous escape artist. He could get out of locked boxes and sealed safes. But he's got nothing on Eli Manning. The Giants' QB made like Houdini in a helmet in Super Bowl XLII.

With little more than a minute to play, Manning was trapped. He was grabbed. The Patriots' defense had handfuls of his jersey. But Eli wiggled and squirmed. He twisted and pulled. And he got free! Then he looked and heaved the ball downfield . . . what happened next? Well, it just might be the biggest catch in Super Bowl history.

HOW'D HE DO THAT?!

While Manning did his escape act, David Tyree was running around, trying to get open. When he saw the ball coming his way, he waited . . . and waited . . . and leaped! He grabbed the ball over his head — and then he grabbed the ball TO his head! Tyree somehow mushed the football against his helmet and held on as he whammed into the turf. What an incredible catch!

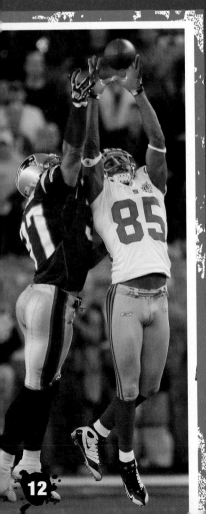

CELEBRATION!

After that, it was almost easy. Manning found Plaxico Burress in the corner of the end zone a few plays later and the miracle was complete. Not only did Tyree's stunning catch set up the winning score, the Giants had upset the Patriots. New England had not lost a game all year. Until they met with Eli Houdini.

RECORD IN RED

Heading into Super Bowl XLIII, Larry Fitzgerald was the biggest story in the NFL. The speedy Arizona receiver was lighting up the stat sheets. By the end of this Super Bowl, he set records for catches, receiving yards, and touchdowns in a postseason. His totals for the Cardinals' four games were 30 catches for 546 yards and 7 scores.

He reached those marks with seven catches and 127 yards in the Super Bowl. And if not for Santonio Holmes, 64 of those yards would have made Larry a legend.

With less than three minutes to go, Fitzgerald found a seam in the Steelers' tough D. Kurt Warner hit the receiver in stride at the 45-yard line . . . and the race was on. No one caught Fitzgerald. He wrapped up a 64-yard TD strike that gave Arizona the lead . . . for a little while. Though the Cardinals ended up losing 27–23 (see "Holmes, Holmes…"), Fitzgerald's play was incredible.

HOLMES, HOLMES IN THE END ZONE!

Sometimes it pays to speak up. Late in Super Bowl XLIII, Pittsburgh receiver Santonio Holmes approached quarterback Ben Roethlisberger. "I want the ball," he said forcefully. "I will make the play." Big Ben listened to the receiver . . . and listened well!

Taking over with less than three minutes remaining, the duo connected on four passes during Pittsburgh's amazing 88-yard march. On first-and-goal from the six-yard line, Big Ben went back to pass. He saw Holmes on the left, and he floated a pass. Holmes leaped . . . and he missed it! "I thought I had lost the Super Bowl," the receiver said. But Big Ben was not through. He still trusted his receiver.

On the next play, Ben fired a laser that would have ended up in the seats—but there was Holmes! Rising up on his tiptoes, Holmes snagged the ball above three Arizona defenders. He held on tight as he fell to the ground. When he got up . . . he was a Super Bowl champion!

INCREDIBLE RUNS

Running with the football has been a part of football since before there was even football! Long before the forward pass was legal and even before football's rules were set, players ran with the ball. Lots of things have changed since then, but one stays the same — a team that runs well will win. Here's a look at how some great runners helped their teams win Super Bowls.

SWEEP FOR SIX

One of the most successful plays in NFL history was the Green Bay Sweep. Two offensive linemen pulled out to one side and cleared the way for a running back. In Super Bowl I against Kansas City, this play shined on the big stage. In the second quarter, from the 14-yard line, tackle Jerry Kramer and guard Fuzzy Thurston headed to the left. Behind them came running back Jim Taylor. Kramer and Thurston cleared a wide path to the goal line, and Taylor rambled through it. It was the first rushing touchdown in Super Bowl history. The Packers went on to win the game 35–10.

FOUR FOR FRANCO

The Pittsburgh Steelers won four Super Bowls in the 1970s. Their famous "Steel Curtain" defense gets most of the credit. But on offense, they had a player who remains at the top of the Super Bowl record books for rushing. Franco Harris ran for 354 yards in those four games, still the most ever for a career. He scored touchdowns in Super Bowls IX, XIII, and XIV. His steady running was a huge part of the Steelers' offensive success. Harris was not the flashiest runner or the fastest . . . but he got the job done. Hail Franco!

MATT PLAYED A SNELL GAME

In Super Bowl III, no one expected the New York Jets to even keep it close, much less to win. But their defense was solid in the first half, and their running game controlled the ball. Midway through the second quarter, the Jets got on the scoreboard first. Matt Snell bulled his way in from four yards out. It was the only score of the half. The Jets added three field goals in the second half, and Snell ended up with 121 yards rushing. New York's 16–7 victory over the Baltimore Colts is still the biggest upset in Super Bowl history!

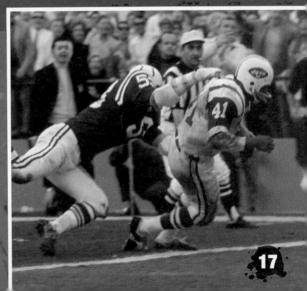

ONE EQUALS 43

In the huddle during Super Bowl XVII, Joe Theismann called the play. The Washington Redskins needed one yard for a first down. Now, on fourth down, he called a goal-line play . . . at the 43-yard line! John Riggins got that one yard . . . and 42 more. Riggins took the handoff and cut left. Miami safety Don McNeal sliced in and grabbed Riggins around the waist. Riggins just kept chugging. He pushed McNeal off and pulled away from the rest of the chasing defenders. Rumbling down the sideline, he went all the way in for a touchdown! The score gave Washington its first lead of the game, and ended up winning 27–17.

FROZEN TOUCHDOWN

William Perry earned his famous nickname for his size. "The Refrigerator" weighed well over 300 pounds. As a defensive tackle, that size came in handy for clogging the line and smashing ballcarriers. But when Chicago decided to give "The Fridge" the football, that size became a battering ram.

In Super Bowl XX, Chicago had the ball on the 1-yard line. In came Perry. Would you want to try to tackle a rumbling 300-pound refrigerator? The Patriots tried to, but couldn't. Perry bounced into the end zone and capped off his big-game score with a thunderous spike.

TWISTY TOUCHDOWN

Marcus Allen was hard to tackle. He had a knack for spinning or twisting or just plain shimmying to make tacklers miss. In Super Bowl XVIII, all his skills were on view. On the last play of the third quarter, he took a handoff and moved to his left. As a Redskins defender zinged in toward him, Allen suddenly stopped and the guy flew right past. Then Allen spun around to go back the way he had come. He ran past another defender and crossed the line of scrimmage. Allen sprinted downfield and two Washington defenders chased him. But no one was going to catch Marcus on that play. His back-and-forth 74-yard run remains a Super Bowl classic.

THE PERFECT NICKNAME

No player ever had a more perfect nickname than Terrell Davis. The powerful Denver running back went into Super Bowl XXXII on a big roll. He gained 1,750 yards that season and ran for 15 touchdowns. (In 1998, he ran for 2,008 yards and scored 21 more times!)

He just kept rolling in the Super Bowl. Against a tough Packers defense, Davis gained 157 yards on the ground. Three of those yards came on 1-yard scoring runs in the first, third, and fourth quarters. The three rushing scores gave him a Super Bowl record and cemented his nickname. What was it? T.D., of course.

GO, WILLIE, GO!

The Pittsburgh Steelers and Seattle Seahawks were locked in a low-scoring game in Super Bowl XL. Pittsburgh held a small 7–3 lead as the second half began. That's when Willie Parker gave the Steelers a bigger cushion and the momentum to win the game.

On the second half's second play, Parker took a handoff and cut to the right. He bounded through a hole made by his blockers, cut past a linebacker, and sprinted past a diving defensive back. As he neared the end zone, he glanced back. He was safe — there was no Seattle player within 15 yards. Parker dove into the end zone to end his Super Bowl record 75-yard run.

DOMINATING DEFENSE!

Have you heard this old football saying: Defense wins championships. In the case of the plays on these pages, that was certainly true! Let's look at the greatest moments in Super Bowl history from the defensive point of view.

LUCKY JACK

"Squirek! Get in the game!" Those words, spoken by an Oakland Raiders defensive coach, created a Super Bowl hero. Playing the Raiders, the Redskins were near their own goal line with just a few seconds left in the first half. Instead of running out the clock, they tried a pass play. The Raiders were ready. That's why backup linebacker Jack Squirek was sent into the game at the last minute. He saw the pass from Joe Theismann, stepped in front of it, and waltzed into the end zone. That made it 21–3 Oakland on their way to a convincing 38–9 win.

THE GREAT WALL OF DEFENSE

The 49ers won four Super Bowls in the 1980s. They won most of them with a high-scoring offense. They won their first, however, thanks to their defense. Late in the third quarter, the Cincinnati Bengals were knocking on the door. A score would inch them closer and turn the momentum their way. The 49ers' defense decided to keep that from happening. On three plays from the 1-yard line, the San Francisco defense stuffed the Bengals. The 'Niners took over and ended up winning the game, 26–21.

BIG BAD BEARS

During the 1985 season, the Chicago Bears defense was dominant. They allowed fewer than 200 points in 16 games. They allowed 10 or fewer points in 10 games! They did not allow a single point in two playoff games to reach Super Bowl XX. In that game, against the New England Patriots, they were Bears on a rampage. They set a Super Bowl record with 7 sacks. They allowed only 7 rushing yards. Yes, 7. In the first half, New England gained minus-19 total yards! It was a wipeout, and the Bears won 46–10.

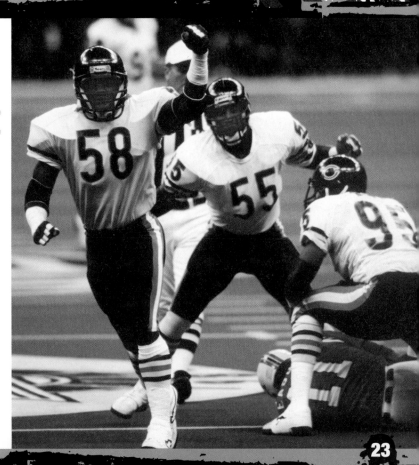

DON'T "LETT" HIM SCORE!

In Super Bowl XXVII, an offensive player made one of the most famous defensive plays ever. In the fourth quarter, big Leon Lett of the Cowboys picked up a Buffalo fumble. He took off for the end zone. Near the goal line, Leon held out the ball in celebration. Bad move. Buffalo wide receiver Don Beebe, though his team was out of the game, never gave up. He chased Lett all the way downfield. Just before Lett got into the end zone, Beebe knocked the ball out of his hand. A TD-saving play and a lesson on never giving up.

ONE IN A MILLION

There must be a million guys named Mike Jones. Heck, six different guys with that name have played in the NFL. This Mike Jones was a linebacker for the St. Louis Rams in Super Bowl XXXIV. His team led the Tennessee Titans 23–16 with just six seconds left in the game. The Titans were on the 10-yard line. A score would tie the game and force overtime.

Titans receiver Kevin Dyson caught a pass and streaked toward the end zone. Up stepped Mike Jones to take his place in Super Bowl history. The linebacker made a perfect leg tackle of Dyson. Though the receiver stretched, Jones held on tight. The game ended with the ball inches from the goal line. It was the only time a Super Bowl ended on such a close play. And it was made by the one and only Mike Jones.

JAMES AND THE GIANT . . . FUMBLE

In Super Bowl XXVII, Dallas beat Buffalo 52–17. A year later, the same two teams met. At halftime, it was the other way around; Buffalo led 13–6. Less than a minute into the second half, however, things got back to normal, thanks to a big defensive play.

Buffalo's Thurman Thomas fumbled. Dallas safety James Washington picked up the loose ball and headed for six. Forty-six weaving, spinning, sprinting yards later, the game was tied and Dallas was on the way to another Super Bowl win.

LONGEST PLAY EVER!

In the long history of Super Bowls, there have been long kickoff returns, long touch-down passes, long runs . . . but none have been as long as the rumble by Pittsburgh linebacker James Harrison in Super Bowl XLIII.

Pittsburgh was trying to keep Arizona from taking the lead as time was running out in the first half. Then Harrison stepped in front of a Kurt Warner pass at the goal line. He saw lots of green ahead of him and he took off running. Both teams took off with him, the Steelers to block and the Cardinals trying to tackle him. One after another, Cardinals players took a shot, but couldn't bring him down.

Finally, as Harrison neared the end zone, Arizona receiver Larry Fitzgerald tried one more time. He grabbed the big linebacker and tried to rodeo-ride him to the ground. Fitzgerald's try was too little, too late. Harrison fell headfirst into the end zone to complete a 100-yard interception return. He had turned the game around for his team . . . and put himself into the Super Bowl record book.

PIRATE THIEVES!

Buccaneer is another name for a pirate. Pirates steal things. In Super Bowl XXXVII, the Tampa Bay Buccaneers lived up to their swashbuckling name. The team set a Super Bowl record by intercepting five Oakland Raiders' passes. They made things worse for Oakland by returning three of those picks for touchdowns. Oh, and they sacked poor Rich Gannon five times, too. Ouch. In the third quarter, Dwight Smith returned one pick 44 yards for a score. Later, Derrick Brooks matched his teammate. Smith wrapped up Tampa Bay's 48–21 win with a 50-yard return score with two seconds left.

GOOD TIMING

Indianapolis defensive back Kelvin Hayden picked a good time to make his first interception in the NFL. He did it during a Super Bowl! It was Super Bowl XLI and the Colts were clinging to a 22–17 lead. The Chicago Bears were driving toward a go-ahead touchdown in the fourth quarter. That's when Hayden made his move. He leaped to snag a pass from Rex Grossman. He tiptoed down the sideline, glided around some Bears tacklers, and found the end zone. The 56-yard score clinched the Colts' victory.

VERY SPECIAL PLAYS!

Special-teams players don't always get the same attention as runners and receivers. But when the big game is on the line, these players can be the difference between winning and going home with tears in your eyes.

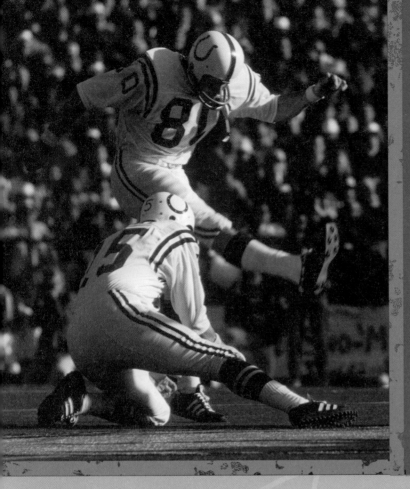

NO PRESSURE!

How nervous was Baltimore Colts rookie kicker Jim O'Brien? He tried to pull up some grass, so he could toss in the air to judge the wind. One problem: the field was artificial turf! Why was he so nervous? Oh, nothing special, really. All he had to do was make a 32-yard field goal with five seconds left to give his team its first-ever Super Bowl victory. Well, he overcame the jitters and made the field goal. Until Adam Vinatieri made a field goal on the final play 31 years later, it was the only Super Bowl with such a late game-winning kick.

TWICE IS NICE

No game puts more pressure on a player than a Super Bowl. And no player feels that pressure more than a kicker. After his team's hard work, it's up to him to make the kick. There are no excuses — you get to be a hero or you all go home sad. In two Super Bowls, Adam Vinatieri of the New England Patriots was the hero. In Super Bowl XXXVI, Adam drilled a 48-yard field goal with no time left on the clock. It gave his team a 20–17 victory over the

St. Louis Rams. It was also the first time in Super Bowl history that the game had ended with a score on the final play. Just that kick alone would have made Adam a legend. And then he did it again two years later.

In Super Bowl XXXVIII, it looked like he was heading for a bad day. He missed a 31-yard kick and had another field-goal try blocked. But with four seconds left, he came through in the clutch. Adam was perfect on a 41-yard kick that gave New England a 32–29 victory over Carolina.

FIZZLED FIREWORKS

Not every Super Bowl play is memorable for a good reason. As good as NFL players are, sometimes things don't work out . . . at the worst possible time. Here are a few stories of some of the biggest "Oops!" moments in Super Bowl history.

NO, GARO . . . NO!

Kickers should not pass the ball. Miami's Garo Yepremian learned that lesson the hard way. In Super Bowl VII, his field goal was blocked. The ball bounced back toward the little guy. Instead of falling on it, he picked it up. He tried to pass it, but it looked more like he was doing the shot put. The wobbly duck he launched was picked off by Washington's Mike Bass, who returned it for a TD. Miami won anyway.

MR. SMITH GOES TO THE DOGHOUSE

Tight end Jackie Smith is in the Pro Football Hall of Fame for his long and successful career. But he has one bad mark on that record. In Super Bowl XIII, he had a sure touchdown pass clang off his chest. His Cowboys lost to the Steelers by only four points. Ouch.

WIDE RIGHT

It would have been a heck of a kick. It would have been one of the longest of the season for the kicker. But he missed it. On the last play of Super Bowl XXV against the Giants, kicker Scott Norwood of the Buffalo Bills pushed a 47-yard field-goal try just to the right of the upright. Bills fans still weep.

SO CLOSE TO PERFECTION

Remember the miracle Giants finish in Super Bowl XLII? It almost didn't get a chance to happen. Just a few plays before David Tyree's wild catch, New England cornerback Asante Samuel could have ended New York's final drive. A pass from Eli Manning went right to Samuel . . . but he dropped it. Had he made that interception, the Patriots could have changed their name to the Perfects.

SUPER BOWL ALL-TIME RESULTS

Game	Score	Most Valuable Player
XLIV		
XLIII	Steelers 27, Cardinals 23	WR Santonio Holmes, Steelers
XLII	Giants 17, Patriots 13	QB Eli Manning, Giants
XLI	Colts 29, Bears 17	QB Peyton Manning, Colts
XL	Steelers 21, Seahawks 10	WR Hines Ward, Steelers
XXXIX	Patriots 24, Eagles 21	WR Deion Branch, Patriots
XXXVIII	Patriots 32, Panthers 29	QB Tom Brady, Patriots
XXXVII	Buccaneers 48, Raiders 21	S Dexter Jackson, Buccaneers
XXXVI	Patriots 20, Rams 17	QB Tom Brady, Patriots
XXXV	Ravens 34, Giants 7	LB Ray Lewis, Ravens
XXXIV	Rams 23, Titans 16	QB Kurt Warner, Rams
XXXIII	Broncos 34, Falcons 19	QB John Elway, Broncos
XXXII	Broncos 31, Packers 24	RB Terrell Davis, Broncos
XXXI	Packers 35, Patriots 21	KR-PR Desmond Howard, Packers
XXX	Cowboys 27, Steelers 21	CB Larry Brown, Cowboys
XXIX	49ers 49, Chargers 21	QB Steve Young, 49ers
XXVIII	Cowboys 30, Bills 13	RB Emmitt Smith, Cowboys
XXVII	Cowboys 52, Bills 17	QB Troy Aikman, Cowboys
XXVI	Redskins 37, Bills 24	QB Mark Rypien, Redskins
XXV	Giants 20, Bills 19	RB Ottis Anderson, Giants
XXIV	49ers 55, Broncos 10	QB Joe Montana, 49ers
XXIII	49ers 20, Bengals 16	WR Jerry Rice, 49ers
XXII	Redskins 42, Broncos 10	QB Doug Williams, Redskins
XXI	Giants 39, Broncos 20	QB Phil Simms, Giants
XX	Bears 46, Patriots 10	DE Richard Dent, Bears
XIX	49ers 38, Dolphins 16	QB Joe Montana, 49ers
XVIII	Raiders 38, Redskins 9	RB Marcus Allen, Raiders
XVII	Redskins 27, Dolphins 17	RB John Riggins, Redskins
XVI	49ers 26, Bengals 21	QB Joe Montana, 49ers
XV	Raiders 27, Eagles 10	QB Jim Plunkett, Raiders
XIV	Steelers 31, Rams 19	QB Terry Bradshaw, Steelers
XIII	Steelers 35, Cowboys 31	QB Terry Bradshaw, Steelers
XII	Cowboys 27, Broncos 10	DT Randy White, Cowboys
		DE Harvey Martin, Cowboys
XI	Raiders 32, Vikings 14	WR Fred Biletnikoff, Raiders
X	Steelers 21, Cowboys 17	WR Lynn Swann, Steelers
IX	Steelers 16, Vikings 6	RB Franco Harris, Steelers
VIII	Dolphins 24, Vikings 7	RB Larry Csonka, Dolphins
VII	Dolphins 14, Redskins 7	S Jake Scott, Dolphins
VI	Cowboys 24, Dolphins 3	QB Roger Staubach, Cowboys
V	Colts 16, Cowboys 13	LB Chuck Howley, Cowboys
IV	Chiefs 23, Vikings 7	QB Len Dawson, Chiefs
III	Jets 16, Colts 7	QB Joe Namath, Jets
II	Packers 33, Raiders 14	QB Bart Starr, Packers
I	Packers 35, Chiefs 10	QB Bart Starr, Packers